400+ FUN & UNBELIEVABLE HOCKEY FACTS FOR KIDS

DISCOVER CRAZY COMEBACKS, DILIGENT DEFENSEMEN, SILLY SUPERSTITIONS & SO MUCH MORE! (THE PERFECT GIFT FOR HOCKEY LOVERS & YOUNG READERS)

HCK PRESS

For my wonderful family. And for you, the Hockey lover reading this book!

CONTENTS

INTRODUCTION

In this gigantic book of facts, you'll discover more than 400 absolutely unbelievable Hockey Facts & Trivia. Armed with this knowledge, you'll be able to impress your friends, family and school mates. You'll also learn tons of important things about Hockey, should you be interested in playing for fun, or competitively.

The chapters span across the history of hockey, the science of skating, hockey sang, generosity in hockey, overcoming adversity, superstitions, times the rules were changed and why, as well as what the future of hockey might look like, and so much more.

The book is split into 20 chapters - but you don't have to read it all at once. Just crack open any page, and be amazed by the facts you see! Many of the facts are shocking, fun and jaw-dropping, while others are informative and educational - whether that's about who holds the goal scoring records or which coach is well-known for his big moustache!

With the introduction out of the way, let's get right into the first chapter - The Early History of Hockey!

1

EARLY HISTORY OF HOCKEY

1. Ice hockey traces back to games played on frozen lakes and ponds in the UK, with evidence of a stick and ball game from the 18th century resembling field hockey.

2. The earliest form of ice hockey was thought to be played by the Mi'kmaq, an Indigenous people in Canada, who had a game called "oochamkunutk," which involved a wooden stick and a ball.

3. Windsor, Nova Scotia, is known as the birthplace of hockey, where the game was first played around the early 19th century by British soldiers stationed there.

4. THE NAME "HOCKEY" likely comes from the French word "hoquet," meaning shepherd's stick, referring to the shape of the stick used to hit the ball or puck.

~

5. The first recorded indoor ice hockey game took place on March the 3rd, 1875, in Montreal, Canada, at the Victoria Skating Rink, with nine players on each team.

~

6. Early ice hockey pucks were made from frozen cow dung, which made for a smelly game! Later, wooden and eventually rubber pucks were used.

~

7. In the 1880s, students at McGill University in Montreal established the first set of formal ice hockey rules, which helped to standardize the game.

~

8. The world's first ice hockey club - the McGill University Hockey Club - was officially formed in 1877, sparking the spread of organized hockey teams!

~

9. The first women's ice hockey game on record was played in 1892 in Barrie, Ontario. The women played with a puck, and the teams were divided by the color of their hats.

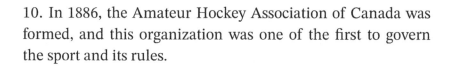

10. In 1886, the Amateur Hockey Association of Canada was formed, and this organization was one of the first to govern the sport and its rules.

11. Ice hockey sticks in the early days were made entirely from a single piece of wood, which often broke, leading to the innovation of laminated sticks for better durability.

12. The original Stanley Cup, awarded to the best hockey team in Canada, was only 7 inches high and was donated by Lord Stanley of Preston in 1893.

13. The first professional ice hockey league was the International Professional Hockey League, established in 1904, featuring teams from the United States and Canada.

14. Ice hockey was first played at the Olympics in the 1920 Summer Games. It was then permanently moved to the Winter Olympic Games when they began in 1924.

15. Early hockey goalies had a risky job; they played without masks until Montreal Maroons' Clint Benedict wore one in 1930 after an injury.

∿

16. Before the Zamboni was invented in 1949, ice surfaces were manually cleaned with shovels and squeegees, a task that could take hours!

∿

17. The National Hockey League (NHL), formed in 1917, originally consisted of only four teams: the Montreal Canadiens, Montreal Wanderers, Ottawa Senators, and Quebec Bulldogs.

∿

18. The 1917 NHL season saw the introduction of the 'forward pass,' which was initially allowed only in the defensive and neutral zones.

∿

19. Ice hockey pucks are frozen before games to prevent them from bouncing on the ice, a practice that began in the early 20th century.

∿

20. The famous hockey phrase "hat trick," meaning three goals in one game by a player, is believed to have originated in

the early 1900s when a Toronto businessman would give a hat to any player that scored three goals or more.

THE CRAZIEST COMEBACKS

1. Daryl Evans was an unlikely hero during the "Miracle on Manchester," striking the decisive blow in overtime that etched his name into NHL folklore, symbolizing the Kings' improbable rally from a five-goal deficit against the mighty Oilers.

∿

2. With their backs against the wall, the Toronto Maple Leafs received a strategic masterstroke from coach Hap Day in the 1942 finals. Benching regulars breathed new life into the team, allowing Sweeney Schriner to emerge as a hero with a pair of Game 7 goals to complete an unprecedented series reversal.

∿

3. Imagine the shock when Paul Cavallini, the stalwart on the Blues' blue line, fired home the game-winner in 1990,

climaxing an improbable surge from a five-goal chasm to stun the Maple Leafs in a dizzying spectacle of determination.

4. It took a returning Simon Gagne to ignite the Flyers in 2010, delivering a fairytale overtime winner in Game 4 and the series-clinching goal in Game 7, ensuring that their fight-back from both the series and a Game 7 three-goal deficit would live long in Philadelphia lore.

5. Ed Westfall wasn't known for his scoring prowess, but with one strike in Game 7 of the 1975 quarterfinals, he turned the tides for the Islanders, completing their comeback from a series that seemed lost and setting the stage for future glories.

6. Sergei Fedorov, aged 39, skated into the history books in 2009, not just by rallying the Capitals past the Rangers but by doing so with a Game 7 winner that crowned him the oldest player to score such a clincher.

7. Andrew Brunette skated into Avalanche history – not for a Colorado triumph, but for a goal that not only capped a Wild comeback but also closed the curtain on Patrick Roy's storied career in a 2003 playoff upset few could have scripted...

8. Dennis Maruk lit the fuse for a North Stars eruption in 1985 with a third-period natural hat trick, transforming a game that seemed securely in the Blackhawks' grasp into a tale of one man's blistering attack turning the tide.

~

9. In 1990, Theo Fleury transformed the ice into a stage for pure theatrics, punctuating an overtime thriller with a goal that propelled the Flames past the Oilers, followed by an ecstatic slide across the ice that has since become part of playoff legend.

~

10. THE "EASTER EPIC" was more than just a game; it was a saga, with Kelly Hrudey's 73 saves for the Islanders underpinning a narrative that culminated in Pat LaFontaine's spinning shot that finally subdued the Capitals in the fourth overtime.

~

11. Patrice Bergeron became the embodiment of clutch in the Bruins' 2013 epic, tying the game with seconds to spare and then winning it in overtime, leaving the Maple Leafs in disbelief and Bruins fans in delirium.

~

12. On one fateful day in 1987, Wayne Gretzky redefined greatness, crafting a masterpiece of eight points against the Nordiques, tying an NHL record and fueling an Oilers comeback for the ages!

∿

13. The legend of the 1972 Canadiens was enhanced by rookie Frank Mahovlich's timely hat trick, serving as the catalyst for a comeback that defied the odds and sent the Rangers packing after a rollercoaster Game 7.

∿

14. A 1993 playoff game became Gretzky's stage as he led the Kings from the brink, his crucial assists in the dying minutes against the Flames turning a potential script of defeat into one of the great playoff comebacks.

∿

15. STEVE YZERMAN, WEARING THE 'C' for the Red Wings, orchestrated a symphony of hockey excellence in the 2002 Western Conference Finals, his hat trick in Game 7 against the Avalanche becoming a crescendo in Detroit's storied hockey annals.

∿

16. AMIDST THE BLACKHAWKS' 2011 comeback odyssey, rookie Ben Smith shone unexpectedly, his Game 6 overtime goal a beacon of hope, even as their storied rally fell just a whisper short in the climactic seventh game.

∿

17. In an 1981 overtime saga, the Sabres showcased a collective resilience, storming back with contributions from

all lines, and it was Gil Perreault who delivered the crucial blow to tie the game and propel Buffalo to an astonishing victory.

18. For the Oilers in 1997, Kelly Buchberger emerged from the shadows, not typically a spotlight seeker, his overtime goal against the Stars not just a winning strike but a testament to the underdog spirit that thrived in the heart of Edmonton.

19. THE SHARKS' 2019 playoff narrative took an unbelievable twist as they capitalized on a controversial penalty against the Golden Knights, with Kevin Labanc steering the ship through a stormy power play that will be recounted for generations.

20. Defying a broken hand, Mario Lemieux's indomitable spirit in the 1992 playoffs was on full display, his critical contributions driving the Penguins not just to victory over the Capitals but towards a championship that would echo through Pittsburgh's halls of fame.

3

FASCINATING HOCKEY EQUIPMENT FACTS

1. As menioned earlier, Hockey pucks were once made of frozen cow dung, a far cry from today's vulcanized rubber discs. This early "equipment" would many times actually shatter in the cold weather, leading to the search for a more durable material for those heated games on ice.

2. Before the advent of goalie masks, brave netminders would guard the posts bare-faced. It wasn't until 1959 that Jacques Plante defied tradition, introducing the first goalie mask after a puck struck his face, revolutionizing the position forever.

3. The curve on a hockey stick blade isn't just for style; it was popularized by Chicago Blackhawks' Stan Mikita in the 1960s. A broken stick led to this accidental discovery, which allowed

players greater control and lift on their shots, altering the game's offensive tactics.

~

4. The Zamboni, the beloved machine that resurfaces the ice, was born out of necessity. In 1949, Frank Zamboni created the first ice resurfacer, saving hours of manual labor and ensuring the ice was perfectly smooth for each period of play.

~

5. The Stanley Cup has a mischievous past of being lost, stolen, and even thrown into a pool. It's also been used as a flower pot, and taken into the sauna! It's the only trophy in major sports that has the names of the winning team's players, coaches, management, and club staff engraved on its chalice.

~

6. Imagine suiting up without a helmet. This was the norm until the 1970s. The last player to skate without one was Craig MacTavish in 1997, marking the end of an era and the full embrace of on-ice safety.

~

7. NHL nets have a unique red light behind them that blinks when a goal is scored, an idea credited to a Canadian businessman, Arthur Sicard. Introduced in 1938, it gave fans a clear signal to erupt in cheers without waiting for the referee's confirmation.

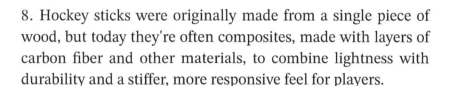

8. Hockey sticks were originally made from a single piece of wood, but today they're often composites, made with layers of carbon fiber and other materials, to combine lightness with durability and a stiffer, more responsive feel for players.

9. Ice hockey rinks are standardized at 200 feet long and 85 feet wide in the NHL, but dimensions can vary in other leagues and rinks. This standardization allows for a consistent playing experience across all NHL venues.

10. Skates once had blades made from animal bones strapped to footwear, but metal blades introduced in the 13th century provided skaters with greater speed and maneuverability, leading to the fast-paced game of hockey we know today.

11. Goalie pads, originally made of leather and horsehair, would absorb water and freeze, making them heavy and cumbersome. Modern pads use lightweight synthetic materials that repel water, allowing for quicker and more agile movements.

12. Professional hockey players often customize their sticks by heating them and bending them to the perfect curve. This

personal touch is akin to a musician tuning an instrument, making sure it's just right for the symphony of the game.

～

13. THE NHL INTRODUCED THE "TRAPEZOID" behind the goal line in 2005 to limit goaltenders' ability to play the puck and thus increase scoring opportunities. This quirky area is often called the "Brodeur Rule" after goaltender Martin Brodeur, known for his puck-handling prowess.

～

14. Did you know the earliest hockey games were played with wooden blocks as pucks? It wasn't until the late 19th century that rubber pucks were introduced, providing a more predictable and less bone-jarring experience.

～

15. Glass surrounding hockey rinks isn't ordinary glass. It's made of a high-impact, shatter-resistant material to protect fans from flying pucks and allow clear views while withstanding the force of body checks.

～

16. Hockey gloves have evolved significantly. Once resembling winter gloves, modern versions provide reinforced protection against sticks and pucks while maintaining flexibility and grip, crucial for those deft passes and stickhandling.

～

17. NHL players go through a staggering number of sticks, sometimes using new ones each game. A player's stick is a piece of finely-tuned equipment, customized to their exact specifications for flex, curve, and grip.

18. A goalie's mask is not just protective gear but also a canvas. Many goaltenders have them custom-painted to reflect personal stories or to intimidate opponents with fierce designs, adding a layer of personal expression to the gear.

19. Have you ever noticed the bottom of a hockey net? It's a mere 44 inches deep, a size that hasn't changed since 1927, designed to ensure that goalies have enough room to maneuver without making it too easy for the puck to slip in.

20. Skate sharpening is a precise science, with players often having their skates sharpened to exact specifications for the right mix of grip and glide. The hollow, or groove, cut into the blade affects speed and turning ability – crucial elements in the fast-paced game.

4

HOCKEY IN EUROPE & AROUND THE WORLD

1. Ice hockey in Europe officially began in the early 1900s. The first European Ice Hockey Championship was held in 1910, with Great Britain emerging as the inaugural winners, a surprising start for a sport now dominated by colder-climate countries.

∾

2. The legendary Russian goaltender Vladislav Tretiak never played in the NHL due to Cold War restrictions. Despite this, he became an icon of international hockey, revolutionizing the style of play for future goaltenders worldwide.

∾

3. In Sweden, the game is so popular that when the national team, "Tre Kronor" (Three Crowns), won the World Championships in 1957, a stamp was issued to commemorate the victory, sealing their heroes in philatelic history.

～

4. Swiss ice hockey has a unique tradition: after the playoffs, the winning team's fans throw teddy bears onto the ice. This celebratory gesture is not just for fun; the bears are collected and donated to children's charities.

～

5. The Czech Republic has a rich hockey history, producing many NHL stars. One of the most significant moments came when the Czech national team defeated Russia to win the gold medal at the 1998 Nagano Winter Olympics, the first to include NHL players.

～

6. Hockey in Norway may not be as well-known, but the country has a dedicated following. The town of Hamar is known for its Viking Ship-shaped arena, built for the 1994 Lillehammer Olympics, combining modern sport with ancient Nordic tradition.

～

7. The Finnish elite league, Liiga, is known for its development of young talent. One unique feature is the "Joker" card system, which allows teams to bring up junior players for a set number of games, fostering the growth of future stars.

～

8. German hockey fans are known for their passionate support. In 2014, the opening game of the DEL (German Hockey League) season was played outdoors, breaking European attendance records with over 50,000 fans braving the cold.

～

9. Italy might be known for soccer, but it has a heart for hockey too. The country's most successful team, HC Bolzano, has competed in both Italian leagues and the multinational EBEL, drawing fans from across borders.

～

10. In Latvia, hockey is the most popular sport. The country hosts the prestigious Riga Cup youth tournament, drawing in future stars from around the globe to compete and showcase their skills.

～

11. Kazakhstan has embraced hockey with vigor, and its club Barys Nur-Sultan is a competitive team in the Kontinental Hockey League (KHL), which features teams from across Eastern Europe and Asia.

～

12. Ice hockey in France has a special highlight called "*Le Match des Étoiles*" (The All-Star Game), similar to the NHL's, featuring a skills competition and a game between the league's best French-born players and international stars.

~

13. Ice hockey in Asia is on the rise, with countries like Japan and South Korea investing in the sport. South Korea's men's national team made their Olympic debut in 2018, an encouraging sign for the sport's growth in the region.

~

14. The United Kingdom's Elite Ice Hockey League (EIHL) has grown in popularity, with teams like the Belfast Giants and Cardiff Devils gaining passionate followings, illustrating the sport's reach across the British Isles.

~

15. The Danish Metal Ligaen is a hidden gem of European hockey, developing talent like Frans Nielsen and Nikolaj Ehlers who have gone on to NHL success, showcasing Denmark's growing influence in the hockey world.

~

16. Spain might be a surprise to some as a hockey-playing nation. The country has its own ice hockey league, and the sport is particularly popular in the Pyrenees region, where teams often cross borders to play French opponents.

~

17. Polish hockey has a storied tradition, with the national team's greatest achievement coming in 1976 when they

defeated the USSR at the World Championships, a victory still celebrated by Polish hockey fans today.

18. The Netherlands has a unique connection to the NHL: the only Dutch player to play in the league, Ed Kea, helped break new ground for Dutch ice hockey on the international stage during his career in the 1970s and 80s.

19. Australia may not be the first country you think of for ice hockey, but the Australian Ice Hockey League (AIHL) is thriving, with the Melbourne Ice and Sydney Bears developing a fierce rivalry *down under.*

20. Ice hockey in China is growing, spearheaded by the Kunlun Red Star team, which joined the KHL to bring a higher level of play to Chinese fans, and with Beijing hosting the 2022 Winter Olympics, the sport's popularity is set to skyrocket.

5

THE SCIENCE OF SKATING

1. Skating on ice is possible because the pressure from the skate blade lowers the freezing point of water, causing a thin layer of ice to melt and creating a slippery surface that reduces friction.

～

2. Hockey sticks are designed using principles of engineering to optimize flex, which allows players to store energy in the shaft during a shot. When released, this energy helps to catapult the puck at high speeds.

～

3. The puck's movement across the ice can be explained by Newton's First Law of Motion: an object in motion stays in motion at the same speed and in the same direction - unless acted upon by an unbalanced force - like a stick or a player!

4. Ice hockey rinks use a specialized refrigeration system that circulates a coolant through pipes under the ice. This absorbs heat from the surface, ensuring the ice stays at the optimal temperature for play.

5. Goaltender reaction times are a marvel of human biology. A well-trained goalie can react to a shot in as little as 150 milliseconds, thanks to highly developed fast-twitch muscle fibers and neural pathways honed by practice.

6. The curvature of a hockey stick blade affects the puck's trajectory and spin due to the Magnus effect. A rapidly spin- ning puck will curve or "bend" in flight, making shots more difficult for goaltenders to predict and block.

7. The unique design of ice hockey skates, with their longer blades, distributes a player's weight over a larger area. This minimizes the indentation into the ice, allowing for smoother and faster gliding.

8. Hockey players often suffer from "skate bite," a discomfort caused by lacing skates too tightly, which compresses the

foot's nerves and blood vessels, illustrating the importance of equipment fitting in sports biomechanics.

9. Zamboni machines don't just clean the ice; they also apply a layer of heated water that fills in any grooves or cuts. This water quickly freezes, creating a smooth surface thanks to the rapid thermal exchange.

10. The boards around a hockey rink aren't just barriers; they are designed with elasticity to absorb impacts. This helps protect players from injuries during collisions, a principle borrowed from automotive crumple zones.

11. Hockey pads and helmets are made using viscoelastic materials, which have both viscous and elastic characteristics when undergoing deformation, providing both comfort and protection.

12. The glass surrounding rinks is made of a polymer called polycarbonate. This material is more impact-resistant than glass, able to withstand the force of a puck flying at over 100 mph.

13. The slapshot, one of the fastest shots in hockey, is a perfect demonstration of conservation of angular momentum. As the player winds up and twists, potential energy is stored in the body, then released into the puck in a fast, whipping motion.

~

14. Synthetic ice, made from a polymer material, is engineered to have a glide factor close to real ice. This allows for ice hockey training in environments where it's not feasible to maintain a frozen surface.

~

15. Stopping on ice is a controlled slide, where the skater uses friction by turning the blade sideways. The skillful use of physics allows players to stop within a fraction of a second, despite high speeds.

~

16. The cold environment of an ice rink is maintained not just for player comfort, but also to control the ice's hardness and brittleness, which are dictated by the temperature and humidity in the arena.

~

17. Goalie masks are made using materials like kevlar and fiberglass, absorbing the shock of a puck hit and dispersing it over a larger area, a concept in material science that keeps the impact force from concentrating on one point.

~

18. The stitching of a hockey jersey is designed to withstand the force and tug of the game, an application of textile engineering ensuring the fabric maintains integrity under stress.

~

19. The color of a hockey rink's surface is typically white, which is achieved by adding a layer of paint between ice layers. This increases the contrast of the puck and lines for players and spectators.

~

20. Protective hockey gear is often treated with antimicrobial coatings to stop the growth of various bacteria, a nod to the importance of chemistry in sports equipment maintenance and athlete health.

6

WOMEN IN HOCKEY

1. Women have been playing ice hockey since the late 1800s. The first recorded women's ice hockey game took place in 1892 in Barrie, Ontario, where female players played in costumes with long skirts, using a puck made of wood.

∿

2. In 1916, Lady Isobel Stanley, daughter of Lord Stanley (of the Stanley Cup fame), was photographed playing ice hockey on the Rideau Hall rink, showcasing women's early involvement in the sport.

∿

3. The 1920s saw the creation of the Ladies Ontario Hockey Association, pioneering organized women's hockey. Despite limited resources compared to men's leagues, these women laid the groundwork for today's competitive play.

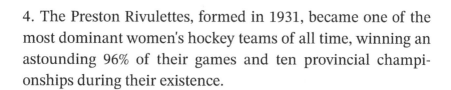

4. The Preston Rivulettes, formed in 1931, became one of the most dominant women's hockey teams of all time, winning an astounding 96% of their games and ten provincial championships during their existence.

5. The 1990s brought significant advancement for women in hockey when the International Ice Hockey Federation (IIHF) held the first Women's World Championship in 1990, with Canada claiming the first gold medal.

6. Manon Rhéaume broke gender barriers in ice hockey by becoming the first woman to play in an NHL exhibition game as a goaltender for the Tampa Bay Lightning in 1992, inspiring countless young girls.

7. Cammi Granato, the captain of the USA Women's National Ice Hockey Team, led her team to gold in the 1998 Winter Olympics—the first to include women's ice hockey as an official event.

8. In 1998, the Canadian Women's Hockey League (CWHL) was founded, offering a professional platform for female

players in Canada, although it faced financial challenges throughout its existence.

~

9. Hayley Wickenheiser, a Canadian, is considered one of the best female hockey players of all time, with four Olympic gold medals and seven World Championship titles to her name.

~

10. Angela James became the first <u>Canadian Woman</u> inducted into the Hockey Hall of Fame in 2010, known as the "Wayne Gretzky of women's hockey," for her prolific scoring ability.

~

11. The USA and Canada have dominated women's ice hockey at the Olympics, with the American team winning gold in 1998, 2018, and 2022, while Canada took the top spot in 2002, 2006, 2010, and 2014.

~

12. Women's ice hockey was almost excluded from the 2006 Turin Olympics due to concerns over competitive imbalance, highlighting the struggles for wider international acceptance and development.

~

13. In 2015, the National Women's Hockey League (NWHL) was established in the United States, becoming the first

professional women's ice hockey league to pay its players, though salaries remain a fraction of their male counterparts.

~

14. The CWHL and NWHL have faced criticism for low player salaries and unsustainable business models, reflecting broader issues of gender inequality in professional sports.

~

15. Noora Räty, hailing from Finland, is widely regarded as one of the best female goaltenders and has competed against male players in Finland's men's leagues, showcasing the growing recognition of women's talent in the sport.

~

16. The Professional Women's Hockey Players Association (PWHPA) formed in 2019 after the CWHL folded, with a mission to advocate for a sustainable professional league and equitable support for women in hockey.

~

17. Kendall Coyne Schofield made history in 2019 at the NHL All-Star Skills Competition by becoming the first woman to compete in the 'fastest skater event', finishing with an impressive time that challenged her male peers.

~

18. Female ice hockey players often have to juggle their athletic pursuits with full-time jobs due to the lack of financial support, underscoring the need for investment in women's sports.

~

19. In 2021, the IIHF held its first Women's World Championship in a bubble due to the COVID-19 pandemic, with teams showing resilience and adaptability in the face of global challenges.

~

20. The rivalry between the Canadian and U.S. women's national teams is one of the fiercest in sports, often culminating in dramatic showdowns at the Olympics and World Championships, pushing the boundaries of women's ice hockey.

7

INCREDIBLE HOCKEY COACHES

1. Scotty Bowman holds the record for the most regular season wins by an NHL coach, with an impressive 1,244 victories. He's also celebrated for nine Stanley Cup wins as a coach with three different teams.

~

2. Herb Brooks, the legendary coach of the 1980 U.S. Olympic hockey team, orchestrated the "Miracle on Ice," one of the most dramatic upsets in Olympic history, when his squad defeated the Soviet Union.

~

3. Joel Quenneville, affectionately known as "Coach Q," is renowned for his mustache as much as his coaching. He led the Chicago Blackhawks to three Stanley Cup victories in six years, cementing his legacy.

4. The first coach to be behind the bench for an NHL game was Art Ross, with the Boston Bruins in 1924. Before this, team captains usually took on the coaching role.

5. Pat Quinn was both a respected player and coach. He earned the nickname "The Big Irishman" and was known for his no-nonsense style, leading his teams to two Stanley Cup finals and coaching Team Canada to Olympic Gold in 2002.

6. Known for his intensity, Mike Keenan earned the nickname "Iron Mike." He coached eight different NHL teams and even won the Stanley Cup with the NY Rangers in 1994, ending a 54-year championship drought for the team.

7. EMILE FRANCIS, NICKNAMED "THE CAT" for his quick reflexes as a goalie, revolutionized coaching by being one of the first to implement morning skates on game days, a practice that has become an NHL staple.

8. Fred Shero, coach of the Philadelphia Flyers during their "Broad Street Bullies" era, was known for his psychological approach to coaching, often leaving philosophical notes in the locker room for his players.

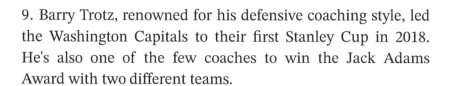

9. Barry Trotz, renowned for his defensive coaching style, led the Washington Capitals to their first Stanley Cup in 2018. He's also one of the few coaches to win the Jack Adams Award with two different teams.

10. Coaches in the NHL often use video analysis extensively, breaking down games into hundreds of clips to analyze plays and improve strategy, showing the high-tech side of coaching.

11. Al Arbour, the long-time coach of the New York Islanders, carried the team to four consecutive Stanley Cup championships in the early 1980s. He was known for his calm demeanor and strategic mind. At age 75, he stepped behind the bench for one game in 2007 - making him the oldest head coach in history.

12. Jacques Demers is the only coach in NHL history to win consecutive Jack Adams Awards, which are given annually to the league's best coach, winning it in 1987 and 1988 with the Detroit Red Wings.

13. Women have been breaking into the coaching ranks of professional men's hockey. In 2020, the Toronto Maple Leafs

hired Hayley Wickenheiser as their Senior Director of Player Development, marking a significant milestone.

~

14. In a move that shocked many, the Pittsburgh Penguins hired 66-year old Bryan Trottier, a Hall of Fame player, as an assistant coach, valuing his wealth of experience in winning six Stanley Cups.

~

15. Toe Blake, as a player-coach, led the Montreal Canadiens to eight Stanley Cup victories. His leadership style emphasized the importance of every player, fostering a team-first mentality.

~

16. Glen Sather, both a coach and general manager, masterminded the Edmonton Oilers' dynasty in the 1980s. His coaching philosophy was built around unleashing creativity, particularly with stars like Wayne Gretzky.

~

17. THE INFAMOUS "TOWEL POWER" phenomenon in Vancouver was started by coach Roger Neilson in 1982, who waved a white towel on a hockey stick in mock surrender to protest officiating, a symbol now used by fans to show support.

~

18. Ken Hitchcock, known for turning struggling teams into contenders, emphasizes a strong work ethic and accountability, which led to him capturing the Stanley Cup with the Dallas Stars in 1999.

~

19. One of the most shocking moments in coaching history came when Philadelphia Flyers coach Roger Neilson was ejected from a game, only to return to the bench wearing a disguise.

~

20. Darryl Sutter, known for his gruff exterior and dry wit, led the Los Angeles Kings to two Stanley Cups in three years and is part of a family with six brothers who all played or coached in the NHL.

8

GENEROSITY, KINDNESS &
GRACEFULNESS

1. During the 2017 NHL Awards, Bryan Bickell, who was diagnosed with multiple sclerosis, was given a heartwarming tribute as he took to the ice one last time to score in a shootout, showing the league's support for his battle.

~

2. THE "TEDDY BEAR TOSS" is an annual charity event held by many hockey teams. Fans throw teddy bears onto the ice after the home team scores their first goal. Each toy is then collected and donated to children's charities. How lovely!

~

3. IN 2016, MONTREAL CANADIENS' defenseman P.K. Subban pledged to raise a massive $10 million for the Montreal Children's Hospital, the largest philanthropic commitment by a sports figure in Canadian history. To date,

more than $6 million has been raised - and the goal should be reached by 2025!

~

4. After the tragic 2018 Humboldt Broncos bus crash, the hockey community banded together in a global show of support, raising millions of dollars and committing acts of kindness in honor of the victims.

~

5. THE "HOCKEY FIGHTS CANCER" initiative, a joint effort by the NHL and NHLPA, has raised over $28 million since 1998 to support national and local cancer research institutions, children's hospitals, and player charities.

~

6. In an act of incredible sportsmanship, Detroit Red Wings player Steve Yzerman handed the Stanley Cup to Vladimir Konstantinov, who was in a wheelchair due to a limo crash, immediately after winning it in 1998.

~

7. Wayne Gretzky, often seen as the epitome of sportsmanship, once purposely missed an empty-net goal to allow a retiring player, whose record he was about to break, to keep the accolade.

~

8. In a remarkable act of kindness, the Ottawa Senators and the Pittsburgh Penguins came together to help save a life by encouraging fans to become bone marrow donors for a staff member's daughter diagnosed with leukemia.

~

9. When Jordin Tootoo, the first player of Inuit descent to play in the NHL, gave his stick to a young fan after a game, the boy's ecstatic reaction went viral, showcasing the impact of a small gesture.

~

10. NHL superstar Sidney Crosby regularly surprises young hockey fans with personal visits and donations, including inviting them to games and giving away signed equipment.

~

11. After 11-year-old fan Anderson Whitehead's mother passed away from cancer, Carey Price of the Montreal Canadiens comforted him in an emotional meeting that was caught on video, showing his compassionate side.

~

12. THE CHICAGO BLACKHAWKS' "One More Shift" program allows former players to take the ice one last time in front of the home crowd, honoring their contributions and fostering a sense of community and gratitude.

~

13. The Willie O'Ree Community Hero Award was created to recognize individuals who utilize hockey as a platform to build character and develop important life skills, in honor of Willie O'Ree who broke the NHL's color barrier.

14. Edmonton Oilers player Andrew Ference organized a surprise pick-up hockey game for a group of children after noticing their rink lacked players, emphasizing the joy of the sport over competition.

15. Mario Lemieux established the Mario Lemieux Foundation for cancer research and patient care after his own battle with Hodgkin's lymphoma, showcasing his dedication to giving back.

16. THE 'LEARN TO PLAY' program, supported by the NHL and NHLPA, provides free equipment and lessons for young children starting in hockey, ensuring the game is more accessible to those from all backgrounds.

17. After the Boston Marathon bombing, the Buffalo Sabres and Boston Bruins fans united in singing the national anthem before a game, in a powerful display of unity and resilience.

18. Gino Odjick, known for his toughness on the ice, also showed his big heart by working extensively with Indigenous communities and children throughout Canada, often visiting schools and encouraging education.

∾

19. When the community of Fort McMurray was devastated by wildfires, the hockey world, including teams, players, and fans, came together to raise funds and provide support for the displaced residents.

∾

20. In a random act of kindness, an anonymous Edmonton Oilers player once paid the grocery bill for a family at Christmas time, showing the spirit of giving is alive in the hockey community.

9

HOCKEY SLANG & TERMINOLOGY

1. When a puck finds its way into the net, players might say the "biscuit is in the basket." Imagine early hockey days when the net was a literal basket, and the puck resembled a biscuit - that's where this saying likely comes from.

2. Aiming high and scoring? That's "Top Cheese," akin to reaching for the best cheese placed high on a shelf. A high goal in hockey is just as rewarding!

3. "BARNBURNER" describes a game so thrilling and full of goals, it metaphorically lights up the arena much like a barn on fire would light up the night sky.

4. Losing teeth on the ice gets a quirky term: "Chiclets." This one's clear—when teeth scatter on the ice, they look just like the small pieces of Chiclets gum.

~

5. Celebrating a player who scores, assists, and fights in one game? That's known as a "Gordie Howe Hat Trick," named after the versatile hockey legend Gordie Howe himself.

~

6. The gap between a goalie's legs isn't just empty space—it's the "Five-hole," a target spot named because it's the fifth basic area that a player can score through.

~

7. Passing the puck to a teammate who scores can earn you an "Apple." Much like sharing a healthy snack, sharing the puck can be just as beneficial!

~

8. Scoring is exciting and deserves a "Celly," which is a shorthand way of saying you've got a reason to celebrate.

~

9. Ever wonder about the guy who makes sure the star players stay safe? He's the "Enforcer," evolving as hockey became a sport where physicality and protection became part of the game.

~

10. "HAT TRICK" might be a common hockey term now for three goals, but its roots are on the cricket field, where a similar achievement would earn a player a new hat.

~

11. A defender not quite keeping up with the play could be jokingly called a "Pylon," much like those immobile orange markers on the road.

~

12. Spend too much time breaking the rules? You'll get to know the "Sin Bin" pretty well, the penalty box where players sit out their misdeeds.

~

13. Sticks were once so rudimentary they resembled "Twigs." This old-school term reminds us of the sport's natural roots.

~

14. The player seated at the end of the bench, rarely playing, has been dubbed the "Grocery Stick," humorously dividing the forwards and defense just like the checkout separator at the supermarket.

~

15. "WHEELING" doesn't just mean great skating; it's also a nod to a player's charm off the ice, especially in romantic pursuits.

~

16. A "BENDER" might sound like a fun night out, but on the ice, it's a less flattering term for a player whose skates lean in as if they're about to snap.

~

17. Do something impressive, and you might be called a "Beauty," a compliment that transcends the ice rink, celebrating a player's skills or actions.

~

18. Every hockey player dreams of making it to "The Show," a glamorous nickname for the NHL, where the bright lights and big cities await the very best.

~

19. Don a full face-shield helmet, and you're playing "Bubble Hockey," giving the impression of being enclosed in your own little world, much like the tabletop game.

~

20. FINALLY, "ZAMBONI" is now the go-to word for the ice-resurfacing machine, forever linked to Frank Zamboni, the

man who invented it. It's a brand, a noun, and a verb all in one!

10

GREATEST GOALTENDERS

1. Did you know goaltenders used to play without masks? It wasn't until 1959 that Jacques Plante made the mask a regular part of a goalie's gear after he took a puck to the face.

~

2. Glenn Hall holds an unbelievable record for goalies — he played 502 consecutive complete games. That's like a goalie playing every minute of every game for over 6 seasons straight!

~

3. Manon Rhéaume shattered a glass ceiling in hockey; she was the first woman to play in an NHL game. Taking the ice for the Tampa Bay Lightning in a preseason game in 1992, she became an instant icon.

~

4. Goalies are known for superstitions. Patrick Roy, one of the greatest, would talk to his goalposts during games, believing they could somehow help him stop the puck.

∼

5. The butterfly style, now a staple for goalies, was popularized by Tony Esposito in the 1960s. This technique has goalies dropping their knees to the ice, forming a "butterfly" shape with their legs to block low shots.

∼

6. Being an NHL goalie is indeed risky. Clint Malarchuk's story is chilling; he survived a skate blade slicing his neck during a game in 1989. His recovery and return to the ice were nothing short of miraculous.

∼

7. The goalie mask has become a canvas for art and personal expression. Gerry Cheevers famously drew stitches on his mask for every puck that hit it, symbolizing injuries he might have had without it.

∼

8. Dominik Hasek, known as "The Dominator," had an unconventional flopping style, often making saves that looked more like acrobatic stunts. This unorthodox method led him to multiple MVP awards.

∼

9. In 1971, a rookie goalie named Ken Dryden led the Montreal Canadiens to a Stanley Cup victory. He wasn't even a full-time NHL player yet, as he was completing law school.

∿

10. Goaltending can be a mental game. Goalies like Martin Brodeur, the NHL's all-time wins leader, credit their success to staying calm and reading the play ahead of time.

∿

11. The shortest goalie ever to play in the NHL was Roy *"Shrimp"* Worters, standing just 5'3" tall. Despite his height, he was known for his agility and was the first goalie to win the Hart Trophy for MVP.

∿

12. The legendary Terry Sawchuk endured many injuries throughout his career. It's said that, by the end of it, he had over 400 stitches to his face before masks were commonplace.

∿

13. Ron Hextall became the first NHL goaltender to score a goal by shooting the puck into his opponent's empty net, showing that goalies can score goals too!

∿

14. Grant Fuhr was the first black goalie in the NHL and the first to be inducted into the Hall of Fame. He was known for

his incredible reflexes and playing an unprecedented 79 games in one season.

~

15. In an act of sheer determination, in 2016, emergency goalie Scott Foster, an accountant by day, played for the Chicago Blackhawks for 14 minutes and saved all 7 shots he faced.

~

16. The most decorated goalie in Olympic history is Vladislav Tretiak, who never played in the NHL but dominated at the international level for the Soviet Union team.

~

17. Billy Smith of the New York Islanders was the first goalie to be credited with a goal in an NHL game, but it was actually an own-goal by the opposing team that he was the last to touch.

~

18. Georges Vézina, the namesake of the Vézina Trophy given to the best NHL goalie each year, was a durable player, never missing a game until being forced to due to illness in 1925.

~

19. EDDIE "THE EAGLE" Belfour was known for his fierce competitiveness and unique eagle-themed masks! He ranks third all-time in wins among NHL goaltenders.

～

20. During the 2017 Vegas Golden Knights' inaugural season, they went through five goalies due to injuries, a surprising challenge for a new team that still made it to the Stanley Cup Finals.

11

DOMINATING DEFENSEMEN

1. Bobby Orr is considered a hockey prodigy; he redefined defensive play by scoring a record 139 points in the 1970-71 season, a feat that remains the highest point tally for a defenseman in a single NHL season.

～

2. Seven-time Norris Trophy winner Doug Harvey was a master on the ice, pioneering the role of the defenseman as a playmaker and showing the hockey world the power of the power play with his exceptional puck control.

～

3. Eddie Shore, a four-time Hart Trophy recipient, epitomized the toughness of hockey, famously continuing to play despite having multiple severe injuries, including a notably brave moment where he played with a broken jaw.

4. Zdeno Chara's towering presence at 6'9" not only makes him the tallest player in NHL history but also created a nearly insurmountable challenge for opponents trying to get the puck past his formidable defensive reach.

5. Larry Robinson, an iconic figure during the 1976-77 NHL season, achieved an astounding plus-minus of +120, showcasing his dominant play which contributed greatly to his team's success during every shift he skated.

6. With a remarkable 26 seasons under his belt, Chris Chelios showcased not just endurance but also consistent skill, setting an example for longevity and fitness in the demanding role of an NHL defenseman.

7. Tim Horton, who is as famous for his coffee chain as his hockey career, was a paragon of strength and toughness on the blue line, often remembered for his robust defensive play.

8. Scott Niedermayer's skating skill was poetry on ice; he had an uncanny ability to move past opponents with an elegance that made him one of the most efficient defensemen of his generation.

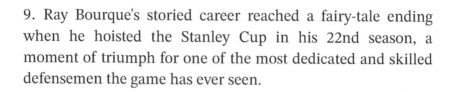

9. Ray Bourque's storied career reached a fairy-tale ending when he hoisted the Stanley Cup in his 22nd season, a moment of triumph for one of the most dedicated and skilled defensemen the game has ever seen.

10. Paul Coffey, second only to Bobby Orr in points by a defenseman, was an offensive dynamo on the back end, integral to the Edmonton Oilers' championship success with his swift skating and scoring acumen.

11. Rod Langway, with a moniker like "The Secretary of Defense," gained fame for his staunch defensive work for the Washington Capitals, often turning the tide of a game with his strategic play.

12. Denis Potvin brought a blend of grit and scoring to the New York Islanders, helping to anchor a team that carved out a dynasty with four consecutive Stanley Cups in the 1980s.

13. The versatile Red Kelly, an eight-time Stanley Cup winner, successfully made the rare transition from an All-Star defenseman to a center, excelling at both positions during his storied career.

❧

14. Renowned for a fearsome slapshot clocked at over 108 mph, Shea Weber represents the modern defenseman's dual threat of physicality and offensive firepower from the blue line.

❧

15. Setting an impressive record, Barry Beck scored 22 goals in his rookie season in 1979, showcasing the immediate impact a skillful defenseman can have on the NHL stage from the get-go.

❧

16. Al MacInnis, recognized for one of the hardest slapshots ever witnessed in hockey, was a key factor in the Calgary Flames' journey to clinch their first Stanley Cup in 1989 with his lethal shot from the point.

❧

17. Nicklas Lidstrom, with a nickname like "The Perfect Human," was celebrated for his unparalleled positioning and decision-making on the ice, which led to seven Norris Trophies throughout his impeccable career!

❧

18. Brad Park was an extraordinary talent on defense, consistently rivaling the legendary Bobby Orr for the Norris

Trophy throughout the 1970s and finishing as a close second six times within that decade.

19. Bill Gadsby, a brave defenseman from hockey's rough and rugged era, endured over 600 stitches to his face during his career, embodying the hard-nosed play and perseverance expected from NHL defensemen of his time.

20. Philadelphia Flyer Tom Bladon stunned the hockey world on December 11, 1977, by setting a record for defensemen that still stands, amassing an incredible 8 points in a single game through a mix of 4 goals and 4 assists.

12

CRAFTY CENTRES

1. Holding the record for the most career points at 2,857, Wayne Gretzky is considered the epitome of a centre in the NHL, earning him the nickname "The Great One."

~

2. Battling Hodgkin's lymphoma and retiring for three years didn't stop Mario Lemieux from returning to the NHL and performing at an elite level, solidifying his status as a legendary centre.

~

3. The youngest captain to hoist the Stanley Cup at age 21, Sidney Crosby, demonstrated exceptional leadership and skill as a centre for the Pittsburgh Penguins in 2009.

~

4. With his signature blend of leadership and timely scoring, Joe Sakic led the Colorado Avalanche as their centre to two Stanley Cup triumphs, defining the era of the 1990s and early 2000s.

5. IN 1969, BOSTON BRUINS' centre Phil Esposito shattered expectations by becoming the first NHL player to break the 100-point threshold in a season, setting a new standard for scoring.

6. Renowned for his prowess in faceoffs, centre Patrice Bergeron often secures puck possession for his team, winning more than 60% of his draws, a skill crucial for any centre.

7. A promise of victory turned into an iconic performance when centre Mark Messier not only guaranteed a New York Rangers win in the 1994 Eastern Conference Finals but also scored a hat trick to make it happen.

8. Overcoming a potentially career-ending ACL injury, Mikko Koivu, centre for the Minnesota Wild, made a remarkable comeback to the professional level.

9. Vincent Lecavalier, a key centre in the Tampa Bay Lightning's run to their first Stanley Cup in 2004, is equally celebrated for his extensive charity work off the ice.

∽

10. The exemplary career of Steve Yzerman spanned 22 years with the Detroit Red Wings, leading them as centre to three Stanley Cup victories and exemplifying loyalty to a team.

∽

11. Not just a centre for the Toronto Maple Leafs but also a Canadian pole vaulting champion, Syl Apps demonstrated the diverse athletic skills that hockey players possess.

∽

12. Diagnosed with diabetes, Bobby Clarke, centre for the Philadelphia Flyers, defied the odds by leading his team to two Stanley Cups in the 1970s.

∽

13. KNOWN FOR "THE FORSBERG MOVE," a spectacular one-handed goal in the 1994 Olympics, Peter Forsberg show-cased the skill and creativity that centres can bring to the game.

∽

14. Bringing diversity to the NHL, Bryan Trottier, a centre with Métis heritage, was instrumental in the New York

Islanders' early '80s dynasty with four consecutive Stanley Cups.

～

15. Eric Lindros, a centre drafted first overall, caused upheaval in the NHL by refusing to play for the Quebec Nordiques, prompting a trade and altering perceptions of player influence.

～

16. Leading the Chicago Blackhawks to three Stanley Cups before turning 30, centre Jonathan Toews is recognized as one of the league's most successful young captains.

～

17. As the NHL's first Slovenian centre, Anze Kopitar has not only made his mark in the league but also expanded the sport's global reach and appeal.

～

18. Jean Béliveau's entire 20-season career as a centre with the Montreal Canadiens is decorated with an impressive 17 Stanley Cups, including his tenure as an executive.

～

19. Breaking new ground as the first European-born player to be drafted first overall, Mats Sundin excelled as a centre and became one of the NHL's most reliable scorers.

20. Renowned for his exceptional fitness, Rod Brind'Amour has set an example for centres league-wide, with a commitment to conditioning that underpinned his lengthy and successful NHL career.

13

THE WILDEST WINGERS

1. Alex Ovechkin, left winger for the Washington Capitals, once stunned the hockey world by scoring "The Goal" in 2006 against the Phoenix Coyotes, while sliding on the ice, facing away from the net, showcasing his incredible skill and creativity.

2. Finnish Winger Jarkko Ruutu is well known for his trash talking, but did you know that **he once bit an opponent?**

3. Known for his flamboyant celebrations, right winger Theo Fleury once slid on his knees the entire length of the rink after scoring an overtime goal in the 1991 playoffs, embodying the exuberance and passion of hockey.

4. Paul Henderson, a relatively uncelebrated left winger, became a Canadian hero by scoring the winning goal in the 1972 Summit Series against the Soviet Union, a moment so significant it transcended the sport itself.

~

5. MAURICE "ROCKET" Richard, the iconic right winger, was so beloved that his suspension in 1955 sparked a riot in Montreal, underscoring the profound connection between players and fans.

~

6. Jaromir Jagr, the Czech right winger renowned for his flowing mullet and exceptional talent, mystified defenders with a signature move known as the "Jagr Salute," a one-handed raise of his stick after scoring, a gesture fans came to adore.

~

7. Brett Hull, a prolific right winger, scored a controversial Stanley Cup-winning "no goal" in triple overtime for the Dallas Stars in 1999, which sparked heated debates and led to a clarification of the league's crease rules.

~

8. Legendary left winger Bobby Hull once shattered a wooden rink barrier with a slapshot, a feat that added to the mystique of his fearsome shooting power and contributed to the NHL's eventual switch to Plexiglas.

∾

9. Left winger Alex Ovechkin made history by being the first player to win the Maurice "Rocket" Richard Trophy, awarded to the NHL's top goal scorer, eight times, showcasing his unmatched ability to light the lamp.

∾

10. In a legendary comeback, right winger Mario Lemieux returned to the NHL after battling Hodgkin's lymphoma, scoring a goal and an assist in his first game back, and went on to win the scoring title in the 1992-93 season.

∾

11. Right winger Jari Kurri once achieved the rare feat of scoring five goals in a single playoff game, demonstrating the offensive prowess that made him one of the most feared players on ice.

∾

12. Right winger Tim Kerr set an NHL record that still stands today by scoring four power-play goals in a single period for the Philadelphia Flyers in 1985, an incredible demonstration of his knack for net-front presence.

∾

13. Right winger Martin St. Louis, undrafted and undersized, stunned critics by leading the Tampa Bay Lightning to their first Stanley Cup in 2004 and winning the league MVP,

showcasing the heart and determination that defined his career.

~

14. Left winger Taylor Hall made a statement by scoring two goals in eight seconds for the Edmonton Oilers in 2013, setting a team record and proving that lightning can strike twice, or in this case, one player can.

~

15. WITH HIS UNIQUE 'SPIN-O-RAMA' move, right winger Patrick Kane has dazzled fans and bewildered goalies, cementing his reputation as one of the most creative and clutch players in the league.

~

16. Luc Robitaille, the left winger, managed an unusual feat by scoring on his first NHL shot, kicking off a storied career that would make him one of the most prolific scorers in league history.

~

17. The inspiring right winger Guy Lafleur, known as "The Flower," once came out of a four-year retirement to play again in the NHL, proving age is just a number and leaving fans and players alike in awe of his enduring talent!

~

18. Right winger Daniel Alfredsson, a leader both on and off the ice, made a controversial statement in 2007 by pretending to throw his broken stick into the crowd, mocking Toronto Maple Leafs' captain Mats Sundin, and fueling the rivalry between the Ottawa Senators and the Leafs.

~

19. Rick Nash, the dominant left winger, showcased his blend of size and skill by scoring a mesmerizing goal against the Phoenix Coyotes in 2008, weaving through the entire team before finishing with poise.

~

20. Right winger Pavel Bure, the "Russian Rocket," once scored a goal directly from a faceoff, catching the opposing team and goalie off guard with his quick release and sharp-shooter precision, a testament to his explosive offensive instincts.

14

SILLY SUPERSTITITIONS?

1. The "Great One" Wayne Gretzky meticulously adhered to his ritual of putting on his left skate, right skate, left pad, right pad, and re-lacing his skates after each period, firmly believing this order was a component of his success.

~

2. Iconic goaltender Patrick Roy's habit of conversing with his goalposts was no secret; he thanked them with a tap for deflecting shots, attributing part of his goaltending prowess to these "supportive" friends.

~

3. Sidney Crosby's superstition extends beyond his birthdate-aligned jersey number; he carries this numerology into various aspects of his career, including contract signings and hotel accommodations, seeking a numeric edge.

~

4. Many hockey players religiously tap their sticks against something solid before games, each having their own set number of taps believed to activate their on-ice prowess.

~

5. Adhering to a specific pre-game meal is a widespread ritual; for Michael Jordan, during his brief foray into minor league baseball where he occasionally participated in hockey skates, the consistency of a steak and potato meal was his game-day foundation.

~

6. Henrik Zetterberg's post-warm-up routine of collecting the last puck from the ice is a personal hallmark, one of the quirky traditions the Swedish player adheres to for game-time confidence.

~

7. In a display of focus on the ultimate prize, players often avoid the conference championship trophy; their eyes are on the Stanley Cup, and touching any other trophy is deemed premature celebration.

~

8. The playoff beard, a bushy symbol of unity and superstition, is a tradition where players forgo shaving to

maintain a streak of luck and camaraderie throughout the postseason.

9. Jersey numbers become part of a player's identity, and their attachment can run so deep that transactions involving significant amounts of money or favors have been made just to secure a preferred digit.

10. Glenn Hall's pre-game sickness was almost as legendary as his goaltending; despite the unpleasant routine, he felt it was intertwined with his mental preparation and on-ice focus.

11. A seemingly small act, like which skate goes on first, carries weight in a player's mind, and for many, disrupting this order is an unthinkable risk to their game flow.

12. Mario Lemieux's pre-game viewing of "Seinfeld" wasn't just about humor; it was a studied choice to keep his mood light and mind clear, readying him for the mental challenges of the game.

13. The avoidance of stepping on the ice lines by goalies is a mix of focus and superstition, a mental game where they navigate an invisible obstacle course en route to their crease.

～

14. Jaromir Jagr's tenure on the ice was marked not only by his prolific scoring but also by his insistence on being the final player off the ice after warm-ups, a solitary moment of preparation.

～

15. Chris Chelios's unique pre-game snack was more than just a meal; it was a ritual that he believed was integral to maintaining his stamina and performance on the ice.

～

16. The art of stick taping is a ritualized process where players channel focus and craftsmanship into every wrap, with some even restarting the process if the result doesn't feel "just right."

～

17. Turk Broda's weight-centric superstitions had him on the scales during every intermission, an unusual tactic to ensure he was in the optimal physical condition throughout the game.

～

18. THE "LUCKY LOONIE" is now part of Canadian hockey folklore, symbolizing hope and good fortune, stemming from the clandestine placement of the coin beneath the ice by a patriotic icemaker in Salt Lake City.

∿

19. Pavel Datsyuk, hailing from a background rich in tradition, would perform a pre-game ritual of scattering snow over his stick, a nod to his cultural beliefs and personal talisman for success.

∿

20. For some players, the ritual leap or series of steps before taking to the ice serves as a physical and mental trigger, priming them for the agility and fortune needed for the forthcoming battle on ice.

15

OVERCOMING ADVERSITY

1. After surviving a harrowing car crash that left him with serious injuries, Mario Lemieux battled back to the ice, defying odds and cementing his legacy as one of hockey's greats.

~

2. Saku Koivu, the former captain of the Montreal Canadiens, made a triumphant return to hockey after a difficult battle with non-Hodgkin's lymphoma, receiving a standing ovation that lasted several minutes.

~

3. Travis Roy, just 11 seconds into his first NCAA hockey game, sustained a spinal cord injury that ended his playing career; he went on to become a motivational speaker and advocate for spinal cord injury survivors.

4. When Jarome Iginla's home was destroyed by a fire during his junior years, he didn't let it derail his dreams; instead, it fueled his determination to succeed in the NHL!

5. Bill Masterton's legacy lives on in the NHL award named after him, honoring his courage after he tragically died from injuries sustained on the ice; the award celebrates perseverance, sportsmanship, and dedication to hockey.

6. Bobby Ryan's childhood was marked by family struggles and his father's legal troubles, but he overcame these challenges to become an NHL star and an inspiring figure for perseverance.

7. Phil Kessel faced criticism over his fitness level early in his career, but he rose above the negativity, went on to become a top scorer in the league, and won the Stanley Cup with the Pittsburgh Penguins.

8. After being cut from his high school team, Martin St. Louis worked tirelessly to prove his doubters wrong, eventually becoming an NHL MVP and Stanley Cup champion.

❧

9. Olli Maatta, at the age of 20, overcame thyroid cancer and returned to play for the Pittsburgh Penguins within two weeks of surgery, displaying remarkable resilience.

❧

10. Pelle Lindbergh's untimely death in a car accident shocked the hockey world, but his memory inspired his team, the Philadelphia Flyers, to a remarkable season as they honored his legacy.

❧

11. Despite losing his brother to a car accident, Dominic Moore stepped away from the NHL to grieve and then returned with renewed purpose, establishing a charity in his brother's memory.

❧

12. Scott Darling battled through the lower ranks of hockey and personal struggles with alcohol to become an NHL goaltender, winning the Stanley Cup with the Chicago Blackhawks in 2015.

❧

13. Tim Thomas took a sabbatical from the NHL to focus on his family and mental health, returning to win the *Vezina Trophy* as the league's best goaltender the following season.

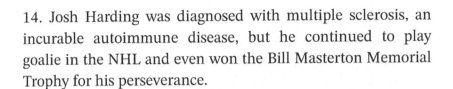

14. Josh Harding was diagnosed with multiple sclerosis, an incurable autoimmune disease, but he continued to play goalie in the NHL and even won the Bill Masterton Memorial Trophy for his perseverance.

15. Bryan Berard overcame a severe eye injury that left him legally blind in one eye; he not only returned to the NHL but also played several more seasons despite the initial prognosis that his career was over.

16. After suffering a stroke at the age of 34, Kris Letang made an incredible comeback to the ice, joining the ranks of the Pittsburgh Penguins to continue his successful career.

17. Jordin Tootoo, the first Inuk player in the NHL, faced cultural barriers and personal tragedies, including his brother's suicide, but he became a role model for Indigenous youth and a speaker on mental health.

18. After multiple concussions and a heart issue, Steven Stamkos faced a daunting road to recovery, but his determination led him back to being one of the most prolific scorers in the NHL.

~

19. Craig Anderson took personal leave from the Ottawa Senators to care for his wife during her cancer treatment; upon his return, he recorded a shutout, an emotional victory for the team and fans alike.

~

20. Rod Brind'Amour, known for his incredible fitness and work ethic, overcame a series of injuries and critics to lead the Carolina Hurricanes to their first Stanley Cup, demonstrating the power of determination and leadership.

16

FORMIDABLE FRIENDSHIPS!

1. When the Pittsburgh Penguins won the Stanley Cup in 2016 and 2017, the bond between Sidney Crosby and Evgeni Malkin was on full display. They celebrated by jet skiing with the Cup, a rare sight that combined victory with pure joy.

~

2. Despite being on opposing teams, Patrick Kane and Jonathan Toews were roommates during the 2010 Olympics, showcasing their competitive friendship by plastering each other's spaces with team memorabilia in a playful rivalry.

~

3. Bobby Orr and Phil Esposito were known for their shenanigans off the ice as much as their play on it. <u>Once, they convinced a rookie he was traded to another team, packing his bags before revealing the joke!</u>

∽

4. George Parros and Kevin Westgarth, both known for their enforcer roles on the ice, shared a love for Princeton University, their alma mater. They co-hosted charity events, proving their brawn was matched by their brains and generosity.

∽

5. After Scott Niedermayer signed with the Anaheim Ducks, leaving the New Jersey Devils, he invited his former teammate Martin Brodeur for a summer of fishing. The two shared a love for the quiet sport, a stark contrast to the fast-paced hockey life.

∽

6. Jaromir Jagr and Mario Lemieux, legends of the game, shared a unique bond. They were known to play practical jokes, including once filling a teammate's car with packing peanuts as a prank.

∽

7. During the NHL lockout in 2012, many players found themselves with unexpected free time. Steven Stamkos and P.K. Subban turned this into an opportunity, creating a comedy skit for a sports network that left fans in stitches.

∽

8. Brad Marchand and Torey Krug became notorious for their holiday costume parties, often shared on social media, where the rest of the Boston Bruins would join in on the fun, dressing up in elaborate outfits.

~

9. Wayne Gretzky and Mark Messier's friendship led to them opening a restaurant together in New York City during their time with the Rangers, a hangout spot that became legendary among hockey fans.

~

10. WHEN THE RED WINGS' Tomas Holmstrom hosted a Swedish Midsummer party, Henrik Zetterberg and Nicklas Lidstrom showed up in traditional garb, complete with Viking helmets, much to the amusement of their teammates.

~

11. Tony Esposito and Stan Mikita of the Chicago Blackhawks once convinced a rookie that his car had been stolen during practice. The car was actually just hidden behind the rink, but it took hours for the poor rookie to figure it out.

~

12. After winning the Stanley Cup, the entire St. Louis Blues team, led by close friends Ryan O'Reilly and Vladimir Tarasenko, took the cup to a local bar and spent the night singing karaoke with fans, creating lifelong memories.

∾

13. Colorado Avalanche's Nathan MacKinnon and Cale Makar, despite their age difference, formed an unexpected duo, often seen battling it out in intense ping-pong matches before games, a ritual they swear by for good luck.

∾

14. Brendan Gallagher and Alex Galchenyuk of the Montreal Canadiens were known to have a 'bromance,' and they famously took it to the next level by appearing in a humorous cooking show segment that had fans laughing at their kitchen antics.

∾

15. When the NHL announced an outdoor game in Los Angeles, friends and rivals Anze Kopitar of the Kings and Ryan Getzlaf of the Ducks decided to promote it by going to the beach—in full gear, skates included.

∾

16. Former Edmonton Oilers teammates Andrew Cogliano and Sam Gagner once embarked on a European backpacking adventure in the offseason, sharing their hilarious misadventures on social media.

∾

17. GRITTY, THE PHILADELPHIA FLYERS' mascot, once received a touching gift from his "best friend" PK Subban – a

customized Christmas sweater, which Gritty wore with pride, showing that friendships in hockey can even extend to mascots.

~

18. After being traded, Phil Kessel made sure to return to Toronto to take his close friend, Tyler Bozak, out for a night on the town, a gesture that Bozak shared on Twitter, expressing his gratitude for the lasting friendship.

~

19. Jamie Benn and Tyler Seguin once entered a Halloween costume contest dressed as the legendary 'Step Brothers' duo, complete with sleepwalking antics that replicated scenes from the movie to entertain their teammates.

~

20. Alexander Ovechkin and Nicklas Backstrom, the dynamic Capitals duo, are not just teammates but also neighbors. They've been known to engage in epic snowball fights, bringing their competitive spirit right to each other's front yards.

17

THE GREATEST FAN STORIES

1. A Detroit Red Wings fan once threw a real octopus onto the ice during the playoffs, a tradition that started in 1952. The eight legs symbolized the eight wins that it took to win the Stanley Cup at the time.

∼

2. In 2010, a Vancouver Canucks fan famously dressed in a green spandex suit to distract opposing players in the penalty box, becoming an instant sensation and part of the 'Green Men' duo.

∼

3. A Pittsburgh Penguins fan saved the life of a fellow attendee who was suffering a stroke during a game. She noticed the signs, alerted the medical staff, and was later thanked by the team and the fan she helped.

4. Fans of the Winnipeg Jets are known for their 'Whiteout' during playoffs, where everyone in the arena wears white, creating an intimidating sea of color in support of their team.

5. A fan of the Montreal Canadiens had his ashes laid to rest in the Bell Centre after his passing, a testament to his lifelong dedication to the team.

6. A San Jose Sharks fan created a massive, team-inspired shark head for fans to walk through entering the SAP Center, enhancing the game-day atmosphere.

7. An anonymous Toronto Maple Leafs fan donated thousands to charity after the team made the playoffs, honoring a promise made on social media.

8. New York Rangers fans banded together to help a fellow fan propose to his girlfriend on the Jumbotron during a game break. The crowd's reaction made the moment unforgettable.

9. A superstitious Philadelphia Flyers fan always brings a grilled cheese sandwich to eat during the game. The Flyers seem to win more often than not when the fan upholds this ritual.

~

10. A Boston Bruins fan started the tradition of waving a rally towel during critical playoff games, a practice that caught on and is now a common sight in many arenas.

~

11. An Edmonton Oilers fan once walked over 550 miles to attend a home game, a journey that took over a month and showcased extraordinary dedication.

~

12. Chicago Blackhawks fans once organized a flash mob outside the United Center, performing a synchronized routine before a playoff game to rally the team.

~

13. THE 'HAT TRICK' tradition, where fans throw hats onto the ice after a player scores three goals, was said to be started by a Toronto fan in the 1940s after buying a new hat to celebrate a player's performance.

~

14. A loyal Buffalo Sabres fan attended over 900 consecutive home games, a streak lasting more than 20 years, becoming a local legend and embodiment of fan loyalty!

～

15. Los Angeles Kings fans raised funds to fly a banner over the Staples Center thanking the team after a particularly memorable season, a grand gesture of appreciation.

～

16. A Florida Panthers fan became famous for throwing a plastic rat onto the ice in 1995 after player Scott Mellanby killed a rat in the locker room and scored two goals that night. It started the 'Rat Trick' tradition.

～

17. An Ottawa Senators fan's homemade sign led to the team adopting a new unofficial mascot, *'Spartacat,'* after it caught the eye of the team's management at a game.

～

18. A Nashville Predators fan once smuggled a catfish into the arena, tossing it onto the ice before a game, a tradition that has continued and added to the team's unique culture.

～

19. During the 2014 playoffs, a group of New York Islanders fans chartered a plane to follow their team to an away game, a show of support that made headlines.

20. After a long drought without a Stanley Cup, a St. Louis Blues fan promised to get a tattoo if the team won. In 2019, when they finally lifted the trophy, he followed through and shared the moment with the hockey community online!

18

WHEN RULES WERE BENT!

1. The "Maurice Richard Riot" in 1955 led to a rule change allowing a goal to count even if the net was dislodged, as long as the puck would have gone into the net under normal circumstances.

∾

2. A 1919 Stanley Cup game was canceled due to a flu epidemic. Since then, rules include stipulations for unforeseen events, with the potential to postpone or cancel games for health concerns.

∾

3. In the 1980s, Edmonton's Wayne Gretzky was so dominant in 4-on-4 situations that the NHL changed the rules, defaulting to 5-on-5 play even after coincidental penalties to minimize his impact.

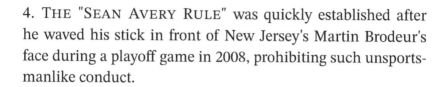

4. THE "SEAN AVERY RULE" was quickly established after he waved his stick in front of New Jersey's Martin Brodeur's face during a playoff game in 2008, prohibiting such unsportsmanlike conduct.

5. After a goal was controversially awarded to the Flyers in the 1975 Stanley Cup due to an unclear crease violation, the NHL refined its rules about goaltender interference.

6. In 1999, Brett Hull's Stanley Cup-winning goal for the Dallas Stars sparked debate as his skate was in the crease. The controversy led to the eventual elimination of the "skate in the crease" rule.

7. The "Too Many Men on the Ice" rule saw a critical moment in the 1979 playoffs, costing the Boston Bruins the game against the Montreal Canadiens and prompting stricter enforcement.

8. Goalie Ron Hextall became the first NHL goaltender to score by shooting the puck into the opponent's empty net in 1987, highlighting the rarity of goalies scoring goals and leading to more goalies trying their luck.

〜

9. In 2005, after a season-long lockout, the NHL introduced the shootout to eliminate tie games, significantly changing strategies and emphasizing individual skill in game outcomes.

〜

10. THE INFAMOUS "TUCK RULE" game in 2002 featured a little-known rule where a player's jersey being tucked into his pants led to a goal disallowance, stirring much debate.

〜

11. A 2014 game between the Detroit Red Wings and Los Angeles Kings ended controversially with a buzzer-beater goal, leading to more precise synchronization between the game clock and the horn.

〜

12. A 1970 rule change was inspired by Bobby Orr's airborne goal to win the Stanley Cup; the league clarified what constituted a legal goal, regardless of whether the scorer's skates were on the ice.

〜

13. THE "CURVED STICK" rule was enforced strictly in a 1993 game when Marty McSorley's stick was found to be illegal, leading to a penalty that allowed the Canadiens to tie and then win the game, influencing strict equipment checks thereafter.

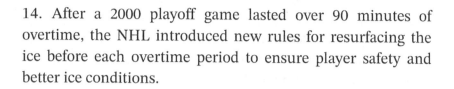

14. After a 2000 playoff game lasted over 90 minutes of overtime, the NHL introduced new rules for resurfacing the ice before each overtime period to ensure player safety and better ice conditions.

15. The tragic death of Bill Masterton from a head injury in 1968 eventually led to the mandatory helmet rule in 1979, though it took over a decade for all players to adopt the safety measure.

16. When a playoff game was delayed due to a power outage in 1988, the NHL adopted the "Emergency Power Rule," requiring backup power sources at all arenas to avoid game cancellations.

17. THE INFAMOUS "HIGH STICK" rule became a hot topic during Wayne Gretzky's 1993 high-stick incident, which was missed by officials, leading to a loss for the Toronto Maple Leafs and subsequent demands for video review.

18. A 2013 game saw a rare enforcement of the "Helmet Rule" when a player's helmet came off, and he continued to play without retrieving it immediately, leading to a minor penalty.

～

19. THE "HAND PASS" rule garnered attention during the 2019 Western Conference Final when a goal by the San Jose Sharks was allowed despite a hand pass, sparking heated debate and calls for reviewable plays.

～

20. The introduction of the "Coach's Challenge" in 2015 allowed teams to contest goals based on offsides or goaltender interference, adding a strategic layer to the game and altering many game outcomes.

19

ART IN HOCKEY & HOCKEY IN CULTURE

1. The iconic "Sweater" by Roch Carrier reveals the cultural influence of the Montreal Canadiens' jersey in literature, symbolizing national pride and the art of storytelling in Canadian hockey.

~

2. The curved design of modern hockey sticks, introduced in the 1960s, not only changed the game but also reflected a shift in design aesthetics towards sleekness and efficiency in sports equipment.

~

3. HOCKEY RINKS' design, resembling a rectangle with rounded corners, is a blend of functionality and aesthetics, providing continuous play without harsh angles that could endanger players.

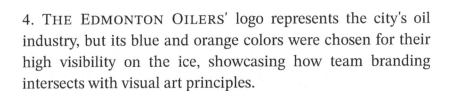

4. THE EDMONTON OILERS' logo represents the city's oil industry, but its blue and orange colors were chosen for their high visibility on the ice, showcasing how team branding intersects with visual art principles.

5. The NHL logo, a shield of silver and black, represents strength and prestige, while the fluid lines suggest speed and movement, blending art with corporate identity.

6. THE RED WINGS' "winged wheel" logo is a classic example of Art Deco influence in sports, embodying the city's auto industry heritage with sleek, streamlined style.

7. Hockey jerseys themselves are a living art gallery, with team emblems and colors representing community identities, historic symbols, and local lore, such as the Chicago Blackhawks' logo, inspired by a World War I military division.

8. The artistic transition of goalie masks from Jason Voorhees-like protection to personalized works of art mirrors the cultural movement of self-expression and individuality in the 1970s.

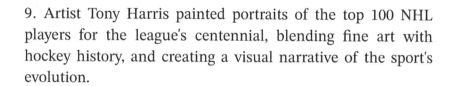

9. Artist Tony Harris painted portraits of the top 100 NHL players for the league's centennial, blending fine art with hockey history, and creating a visual narrative of the sport's evolution.

10. The Stanley Cup, with its layered bands and silver sheen, is not just a trophy but a masterpiece of silversmith art, with each band telling the story of triumphs and defeats.

11. Hockey trading cards are miniature pieces of art, capturing the essence of players and memorable moments, their designs reflecting the graphic trends of their respective eras.

12. The Zamboni, while functional in resurfacing ice, has become an iconic image in hockey culture, often featuring artistic advertisements that glide along the ice between periods.

13. THE VANCOUVER CANUCKS' "Orca" logo is a nod to the indigenous art of the Pacific Northwest, merging cultural art with team branding.

14. Hockey's influence on cinema is highlighted in the artful storytelling of films like "Miracle" and "The Mighty Ducks," which portray the game's beauty and drama.

15. The Montreal Forum, historic home of the Canadiens, was known for its Art Deco architecture, blending the artistry of design with the spirit of hockey.

16. THE "MIRACLE ON ICE" in 1980 was commemorated by artist Daniel Moore in a vivid painting, capturing the patriotic fervor and athletic triumph in a moment frozen in time.

17. Renowned artist LeRoy Neiman's vibrant paintings captured the speed and energy of hockey games, his expressionist style offering an artistic lens through which to view the sport.

18. The annual Winter Classic outdoor game is not only a sporting event but also a visual spectacle, marrying the art of stadium design with the nostalgia of pond hockey.

19. Canadian postage stamps have featured hockey themes, including legendary players and iconic moments, reflecting the sport's cultural impact and its intersection with graphic arts.

20. Hockey's influence on music is evident in "The Hockey Song" by Stompin' Tom Connors, an auditory art piece that has become an anthem in arenas, celebrating the game's place in cultural identity.

20

THE FUTURE OF HOCKEY!

1. Imagine stepping onto the ice and finding your skates adjusting to the rink's conditions instantly. Skates of the future may come equipped with smart technology, automatically optimizing blade sharpness and contour for peak performance.

～

2. Future hockey arenas might be marvels of sustainability, featuring translucent ice from thermochromic materials that change color to indicate temperature, reducing energy use for cooling while adding a visual spectacle to the game.

～

3. PLAYERS' sticks could soon have embedded sensors that analyze shooting technique, providing instant feedback on the flex, angle, and force—revolutionizing training and in-game analysis.

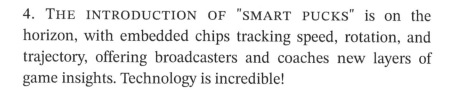

4. THE INTRODUCTION OF "SMART PUCKS" is on the horizon, with embedded chips tracking speed, rotation, and trajectory, offering broadcasters and coaches new layers of game insights. Technology is incredible!

5. Virtual Reality might evolve to allow fans to experience games from the perspective of their favorite players, providing a full 360-degree view of the on-ice action from anywhere in the world.

6. In the quest to prevent injuries, researchers are working on creating responsive gear that hardens on impact, using non-Newtonian fluids or smart materials to offer dynamic protection.

7. The NHL could be leading a global initiative, where countries without natural ice have access to modular, synthetic rinks, expanding hockey's footprint worldwide.

8. Tomorrow's helmets might include heads-up displays, showing players vital game stats and tactical information without taking their eyes off the play.

9. Ice resurfacing could be transformed by laser technology, efficiently smoothing the ice in a fraction of the time, ensuring optimal playing conditions throughout the game.

10. Genetic profiling may become integral to the sport, allowing for a highly individualized approach to training, recovery, and nutrition that maximizes each player's genetic potential.

11. Augmented reality could revolutionize coaching, with holographic displays replacing whiteboards for illustrating plays, turning the bench into a high-tech strategy hub.

12. The fusion of AI and game strategy might give rise to virtual coaches, offering real-time predictive analytics, and personalized game plans, challenging the traditional role of coaches.

13. Bioluminescent technology could be integrated into hockey jerseys, illuminating players dynamically during night games or power plays, adding a new dimension to the spectator experience.

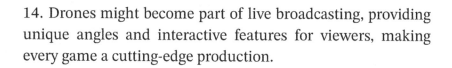

14. Drones might become part of live broadcasting, providing unique angles and interactive features for viewers, making every game a cutting-edge production.

15. We could see the rise of intercontinental leagues, where air travel is so fast that teams could play in multiple countries in a single week, truly globalizing the sport.

16. The advent of hologram referees could ensure flawless call-making, with AI processing every angle of the game, virtually eliminating human error from officiating.

17. Player benches could be equipped with biometric monitoring systems, analyzing and providing health data in real time, ensuring player well-being is continuously monitored.

18. The NHL's philanthropic reach might extend to space, with special matches held at zero gravity in orbital stations, making hockey the first sport to literally go above and beyond... Ok, maybe not soon, but one day!

19. The evolution of ice skates may incorporate nanomaterials, offering unparalleled durability and self-sharpening blades, so players can focus less on equipment and more on the game.

∼

20. Arena experiences could be amplified with immersive 4D effects, including seat vibrations and arena-wide temperature changes, making fans feel every hit and chill from the ice. How cool would that be!?

CONCLUSION

That brings us to the end of our Hockey fact book!

Which chapter was your favourite? Maybe you're a winger, so you loved that one; or maybe you're a science-lover and you found that chapter the most interesting!

We really hope you enjoyed reading this fact and trivia book. If you did, please feel free to leave us a kind review on Amazon.

Make sure to share the most fascinating facts with your friends and family! We plan on making more Hockey books very soon - so be sure to follow our author page on Amazon!

If you have any questions, comments or concerns - please email us at hockey.o2gtr@simplelogin.com

We wish you the best of luck in your future - whether that be Hockey related - or something completely unrelated. Much love, HCK Press!

GRAB OUR NEXT HOCKEY BOOK!

Incredible Hockey Short Stories for Kids

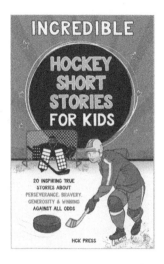

20 Inspiring True Stories About Perseverance, Bravery, Generosity & Winning Against All Odds

Scan the QR code below to buy on Amazon now!